S0-CDV-762

The Gift and the Giver

AMELIA BISHOP
AUTHOR AND PHOTOGRAPHER

BROADMAN PRESS • Nashville, Tennessee

© Copyright 1984 • Broadman Press
All rights reserved
4251-06
ISBN: 0-8054-5106-4
Dewey Decimal Classification: 242.6
Subject Heading: MEDITATIONS
Library of Congress Catalog Card Number: 84-2796
Printed in the United States of America

Unless otherwise noted, Scripture quotations are from the King James Version of the Bible.

Scripture quotations marked (GNB) are from the *Good News Bible,* the Bible in Today's English Version. Old Testament: Copyright © American Bible Society 1976; New Testament: Copyright © American Bible Society 1966, 1971, 1976. Used by permission.

Scripture quotations marked (NASB) are from the *New American Standard Bible.* Copyright © The Lockman Foundation, 1960, 1962, 1963, 1968, 1971, 1972, 1973, 1975, 1977. Used by permission.

Scripture quotations marked (TLB) are from *The Living Bible.* Copyright © Tyndale House Publishers, Wheaton, Illinois, 1971. Used by permission.

Library of Congress Cataloging in Publication Data

Bishop, Amelia.
    The gift and the giver.

    1. Women—Prayer-books and devotions—English.
I. Title
BV4844.B55   1984   242'.643   84-2796
ISBN 0-8054-5106-4

Contents

 Beginnings

IN GRATITUDE TO GOD

For the formative influences of earlier years:
Childhood—My parents,
                Alice and Walter P. Morton
Young Adulthood—Mary Lee Vines Miller
                The J. D. Greys
                Jinks Mahnker
                Floy Barnard
For the sustaining influence of a thirty-year friendship:
Eula Mae Henderson, sister in Christ and colaborer;
For loving influences—My family,
                Ivyloy, Dan, and Judi Lee;
                My friends.

"The lines are fallen unto me in pleasant places;
yea, I have a goodly heritage" (Ps. 16:7)

1  The Gift

The doorbell chimed
Suddenly,
Slicing the room with sound.
My neighbor stood in the doorway;
"Special delivery," she called out
And thrust a package toward me.
"I told someone I'd drop this off,
But it's a surprise
You can't open it till Saturday."
She grinned and was gone.
I stood there, looking down at the package,
Turning it over in my hands,
Wondering . . . wondering.

> Every good gift and every perfect gift is from above, and cometh down from the Father of lights (Jas. 1:17a).

What is that in your hands?

It is a gift.

Gifts may come with form or formlessness, packaged or unpackaged, seen or unseen.

"Every good gift and every perfect gift is from above."

God gives many gifts, some we recognize, some we don't. Life itself and life eternal are gifts. Love itself and love eternal are freely given. The little pleasures that brighten our days, the tasks that stretch us and make us grow, the opportunities that peek out at us from some unsuspecting corner are gifts.

Yet there is one special package we may not recognize as a gift. It is the gift of today. It is decidedly different. It is handmade. For God, who set the sun in the sky and structured time itself, has given it to us. It comes as a basic part of every gift because all that shall be ours today will be sheathed in some segment of it. Yet to each of us it also comes as a gift that stands alone—twenty-four hours, wrapped separately and then bound together in one package labeled *Today*. No portion of it can be opened ahead of time.

We may take each hour and create substance with it. The hour passes, but the substance remains, casting, perhaps, a lengthening shadow as time authenticates and multiplies our efforts. Or perhaps the hour passes, and nothing remains, neither substance nor shadow. That which was not created cannot cast a shadow. Nothing.

Today. It can be used or misused. It can be invested or thrown away. It has no strings. That means you and I may spend it as we wish, but it also means we cannot pull it back once it has slipped away.

What is that in your hand?

It is the gift of today, the gift of time. To have time is to have life. To spend time is to spend life.

This is God's gift to us.

Today.

2 Getting Started

I am disgusted with something—
*   Make that "someone"—*
*   Me.*
I told myself three months ago I'd start
a regular reading program
*   And clean out closets*
*   And write more letters,*
Yet here I sit. I haven't done any of it.
*   I feel guilty.*
What's the matter with me?
Why don't I get these things done?

You must do this, because you know that the time has come for you to wake up from your sleep. For the moment when we will be saved is closer now than it was when we first believed (Rom. 13:11, GNB).

It has been more than twenty years, yet I can see her as if it were yesterday. Her name was Claudia. She was a tall, graceful woman in her mid-forties who frequented a favorite restaurant of mine in New Orleans. She was always well-mannered, well-groomed, and never completely sober.

Enveloped in a rosy glow, Claudia would glide into the patio, and, on occasion, she accepted our invitation to join us. No matter where the conversation started, it always wound around to the same dialogue:

"I really must start tomorrow," Claudia would say.

"Start what?" we would ask, knowing the answer.

"Practicing. I'm a dancer, you know, and I need to get back in shape before I go back to New York. I really must start tomorrow." And she would nod her head slowly, positively, as she reached for her glass of wine.

In the years I knew her, tomorrow never arrived for Claudia. But there were twenty years of saying "I really must start tomorrow." I grieved for her, but I could not pierce the wine-colored haze that clouded her days.

The pattern, however, is by no means confined to those for whom alcohol is a problem. Many of us darken our own days by the shadows of things yet undone. Our intentions are commendable; our performance is not.

Why?

Sometimes a search for answers involves more questions. Let's look at it individually and personally. Is the task really something you want to do, or does it just come in the nice-idea category? And if you really want to do it, are you willing to give time to it?

Seemingly, the "someday projects" are always shoved aside by the here-and-now tasks that demand attention. They float along on a sea of good intentions, unanchored by a time slot. On the other hand, the shopping to be done before Christmas, the costume which must be made before the Halloween carnival, even tonight's dinner, all have time slots.

The project, the task, the responsibility that darts in and out of your consciousness needs to be anchored with a time slot, a specific hour for performance.

After all, we get done what we spend our time doing.

3 New Directions

Today on the calendar looks like any other day—
  A dark number on a white space
  Cozily surrounded by other numbers
  Same size, same color.
But I have the feeling it's a different day.
  Changes are coming.
I'm not exactly scared;
  But I feel like pulling back,
  Avoiding the unknown.
Yesterday was comfortable.
  I liked it.

Be glad for all God is planning for you. Be patient in trouble, and prayerful always (Rom. 12:12, TLB).

We are map lovers. Maps and blueprints and charts. We want one for the road, one at home, and one in the office. We're comfortable. We're "safe."

We accept these visual aids, and we understand they may provide direction, but not necessarily ultimate destination. We may decide to journey farther than the map shows; we may opt to add more to the house than the original blueprint includes; we may pursue a further goal than the chart showing professional growth indicates.

But here's an interesting thing: when we decide to do more or to go farther, we are usually excited and happy about it. We get a new map, draw up a new blueprint or chart, and joyfully go on our way, challenged by ever-expanding horizons.

Except in the realm of the spiritual. Then "that which we cannot actually see" tends to become a problem.

It may be that while we happily sit putting together all the mythical pieces of the familiar jigsaw puzzle, we suddenly encounter a strange-looking piece. It's new. It's totally unfamiliar. Where did that come from? We want to reject it because it doesn't seem to blend in with the rest of the picture, but we have the feeling it fits in somewhere.

Here we sit with the strange-looking piece in front of us. We must do something. Our options are to throw it away, to sit and do nothing, bemoaning the fact that "life" gave it to us, or to realize we may have encountered a part of a new and exciting "picture." It may be only slightly different from the one we know; it may be an entirely different landscape.

God's maps are infinitely superior to ours, though they may be seen only in part by human eyes with limited vision. Why do we feel that we must see the entire picture, that we must understand how each new and different piece fits into the distant diorama? Actually, all we have to do is follow step by step a trip charted by a perfect Mapmaker.

Not only do God's maps lead us in the right direction but also they are well balanced along the way: good days to enjoy, hard times that strengthen our faith and our patience, people to love us and whom we love, and opportunities to minister.

Isn't that, after all, the essence of what we want?

And incidentally, what is that in front of you? You make the decision.

4   God's Timing

I've got this problem that nags at me.
    Usually it roams around in the backroads
        of my mind,
    Then it leaps forward again,
And I'm tired of it. I want an answer.
In fact, why don't I have it already?
    I've prayed about it.
    I've given it to the Lord.
    I've sought the open doors but they all shut.
    Every one. Whoosh.
And I'm still here. So is the problem.
    Unanswered.

> Trust in the Lord with all thine heart; and lean not unto thine own understanding. In all thy ways acknowledge him, and he shall direct thy paths (Prov. 3:5-6).

She was a homemaker in her thirties, warmhearted, loving, and attractive. Active in her church and in community affairs, she was sometimes a model for the young marrieds. "She's something else," they would say. "She takes good care of her husband and children, she works part time, and I've never seen anyone with such patience. She must have been born with it!"

She wasn't. Patience came in a jelly glass. Or with one.

"From childhood, I never had trouble getting things done, at least my part of them," she related. "I guess the good Lord just blessed me with energy. But I want to see quick results, or at least I used to. You know, if you pray hard enough and work hard enough, that ought to do it. You should see results, and you should see them now. If you don't, just double up and try twice as hard. But I found out it doesn't work that way.

"You know how jelly glasses become tea glasses when dollars are limited and baby clothes expensive? Well, one day several years ago we were having company unexpectedly—that is, they were coming in about two hours. And I lacked one glass of having enough. So I finished up what was left of the jelly and went to the sink to get the label off the glass. Using hot water and soap, I scraped and scraped, and got very little results. In frustration, I plopped the glass into a pan of warm water and left it. An hour later, I came back. The water had cooled. The label slid off when I lifted the glass."

It was a matter of timing.

"I guess I learned a great deal from that simple lesson," she concluded. "I could scrape and stew and mutter and fret, and perhaps force the issue. Or I could recognize that certain circumstances known to God have to evolve before a solution or an answer comes."

To carry our problem to the Lord, to submerge it in prayer, points us in the right direction. Unburdened, we then continue our pilgrimage with a lighter step, confident that down the road is the solution we seek, visible when God's time and circumstances have structured the answer.

God's time.

 Reaching

5  Growing

Early morning in the mountains—
Misty, cool, hushed—
The silence unfurls across the treetops
And sifts down into the valley.
I sit quietly on the cabin porch
Wrapped in a soft blanket,
Soaking up the silence.
Has it been a year since I was here?
The calendar says so.
The little pine trees say so.
They've grown.
A year, and the trees have grown,
Have I?

> But grow in the grace and knowledge of our Lord and Savior Jesus Christ (2 Peter 3:18*a*, NASB).

"When are you going to grow up?" The teenager's voice cut across the girls' gym to her friend doing antics on the other side.

"I wish I knew," the chubby jokester called back, gazing down at her hips. "All I seem to do is grow out!"

Perhaps both directions are involved in growing. Grow up, grow out. And it's not confined to young people.

"More than anything else," the frustrated woman exclaimed, "I want to grow as a Christian. I want to, desperately. But all I seem to do is putter around in a fog, going in circles. I'm beginning to wonder, is there such a thing as trying too hard?"

Yes, perhaps there is. Or maybe it is trying in the wrong direction. Perhaps we are trying to collect those qualities that make for growth by a planned and disciplined pattern of behavior. We are trying to "add on" by our own efforts. It doesn't work; it doesn't ring true. Spiritual growth comes in different coin. It is not a collection; it is an offering.

We do not collect patience, caring, kindness, like layers of garments to be donned at the proper time, but rather we offer ourselves to the leadership of the Holy Spirit on a continuing and continual basis. An offering, first. Then an openness.

We must come to our encounter with him with empty hands, having set aside prejudice, preconceived ideas, negative attitudes. Then we are open to new pathways across the familiar landscapes of our todays.

We offer ourselves. We are open to his leadership. Then quietly and confidently, with a peace we had not known before, we step forward. And the fog retreats before our advancing footsteps. Suddenly the day is clear. Quite accidentally, we catch a glimpse of our shadow as we move along and are surprised to notice that it is taller. It is not the position of the sun; it is the position of the Son.

What happened? In offering ourselves, in opening ourselves to the leadership of the Holy Spirit, we have been stretched to new dimensions.

In growing up, in growing out, growth is an "inside job."

6  The Personal Touch

The day stretches out before me—
   Long, slender hours
   That somehow melt together.
   They run through the clock
   And become yesterday.
But not yet. It's today;
   I'm a part of this day
It looks ordinary,
      But it may not be.
      It may be quite different,
      Even extraordinary.

> May you always be doing those good, kind things which show that you are a child of God (Phil. 1:11a, TLB).

An old song tells the story of an elderly lamplighter with snowy white hair who went from lamppost to lamppost, leaving behind him a trail of light. His job was a small one as important positions are rated. But, as the song goes, "He made the night a little brighter."

A small job? Not necessarily. Who can measure the good that comes into the world when a light is lit in a darkened corner. Sometimes just one small light is all it takes. But someone has to light it.

Darkness may come in many forms, some literal, some symbolic. Some may be genuine; some imagined. But, in each instance, it is painfully real to the one struggling in the shadows, reaching this way and that with little sense of direction.

"Lighting the light" may be a friendly phone call, a brief visit, a short note. It may be a chance encounter on the street. The form it takes is not important; the message it transmits is vital.

One observant Christian woman became an effective "lamplighter" simply by verbalizing her interest in others. "I can't really remember when I started," she explained. "But I guess what I do is a sort of pattern: when I meet someone, I shift my mental gears and recall exactly what his or her circumstances were the last time we met or what may have happened in the meantime. I don't just say 'Hello, how are you?' because that's so impersonal. I focus in on their activities, aspirations, or concerns. I comment on these things, or inquire about them, because I am truly interested and I want them to know I care."

Reaching outward, structuring that reach into some form of meaningful communication lights the lamp. It may begin a tiny glow; it may become a blaze that illumines the world.

Who first showed an interest in Marie Curie of scientific research fame and encouraged her? Who reached out to touch William Booth of the Salvation Army and affirmed him in his dreams? Who lit the lamp or fanned the flame for Helen Hayes or John Glenn or Marian Anderson?

Look around you. Who showed an interest in the grocer, the switchboard operator, the baker, the law student, the struggling widow with three children? The light that is lit at a significant time may not someday blaze across the world, but it will lighten a dark corner of someone's life. And who is to say which is the greater?

Someone has to light the lamp. "He made the night a little brighter." An ordinary day may become an extraordinary one indeed. For someone.

7 A Different You

Today I have a good case of the blahs.
I am neither hot nor cold,
    Neither sad nor mad,
    Neither hurt nor happy.
I have no particular desire to do anything
Or to refrain from doing anything,
    Except everything.
Out there somewhere are rivers to ford,
    Mountains to climb,
    Deserts to cross.
But I'm in here. Boxed in by me.

Don't copy the behavior and customs of this world, but be a new and different person with a fresh newness in all you do and think. Then you will learn from your own experience how his ways will really satisfy you (Rom. 12:2, TLB).

Her name was Rachel, and she was totally unforgettable. But not at first. In the early days, it was hard to tell she was there. Light brown hair, hazel eyes, a bit shy, she was melt-into-the-wall average.

The change did not happen overnight. Gradually I became aware of a soft glow about her, like a misty sunrise infusing the landscape with light. That was Rachel.

One day, when her self-confidence seemed strong enough to bear the burden of questions, I talked with her about it.

"What's happened to you? Do you know something I don't?"

She smiled in her gentle way. "No, I'm just learning to act on something that's been there all the time." Rachel went on to explain how dissatisfied she had become with her humdrum life. No big problem. Neither hot nor cold. Lukewarm. "Then one day, reading Romans 12, it dawned on me I didn't have to be this way. God could give me a fresh newness in all I do and think, and that would make a new me. But I would have to do my part.

"The idea of God's changing people is certainly not new. I've heard it all my life. But what I had not understood was that I had to act upon it, I had to do it deliberately, before it could actually happen. I had to ask God to transform my mind, to help me think positive, loving thoughts. And I also had to work at keeping out the negative things that box me in."

Warming to her subject, she put her hand on my sleeve. "Negative thoughts are not just 'I can't do it.' They're also resentment, jealousy, envy, things like that. They're mental tigers; and if you let them roam around unleashed in your mind, they'll eat up everything good in sight and dominate you. Replace them deliberately with what you *can* do and with the thoughts Paul talked about: love, joy, peace, and so on. Remember, the key word is *deliberate*.

"It's like being in love. You don't know what it's all about until you take the plunge and experience it yourself. We are transformed when our patterns of thinking are changed. The whole world looks different. It's not, of course; we are."

Rachel was deliberately and decidedly different. God said it. She believed it. She did it.

8  Habits

A cup of steaming coffee sits before me,
    Freshly brewed,
    Aromatic.
I reach for the cream,
    Pour it in,
    Stir it automatically.
Then my mind snaps to attention.
    Why did I do that?
    I'm on a diet.
Habit, I guess—
    Not thinking.
    I guess I'm "programmed."
That's kind of scary.
Who programmed me?
    Me, maybe?

Thine ears shall hear a word behind thee, saying, This is the way, walk ye in it (Isa. 30:21a,b).

"I've been in this business a long time," said the vocational counselor, "And one paradoxical fact keeps popping up: the young people who succeed are many times not the ones with the most talent. The ones who make it are the ones with the habit of persistence."

The habit of persistence. Habits. How relevant are they in the computer age?

"We can program a computer to do exactly what we want it

to. Too bad we can't program ourselves!" This comment, spoken in jest, carries within it the seeds of truth that stir uncomfortably in the soil of our consciousness.

"Too bad we can't program ourselves." We can, and we do more often than we realize.

Habit is a pattern of thinking, feeling, or acting, repeated so many times that we subsequently do it automatically. But what we are seeing is the tip of the iceberg. What we may not realize is that behavior can be "computered."

Habits are tools that will work for us or against us. When we learn this, we must look at what lies below the surface: we create our own habits by decision or by default. To put it another way: those habits not created by decision will be created by default.

The farmer sweated and strained helping his hired hands dig a ditch. "Why bother with something like that in weather like this?" he was asked. "Why not wait until it gets a little cooler?"

"I really don't have any choice," was the reply. "If I don't dig a ditch now where I want the water to go, it will find its own course. And it may not be where I want it. It's going to go somewhere; and if I don't decide, it will!"

The input of a computer governs the output. The first is deliberate, the second automatic.

I prefer to determine the "input" of my "personal computer" by deliberate decision. God being my helper, this I will do until it becomes habit.

I prefer to reject the path of least resistance, flowing with the tide. Default. "Water will go somewhere. If I don't decide, it will!"

 Understanding

9 Getting Along

I'd rather forget what happened today.
I was downtown, hurriedly shopping
And I met "one of those,"
> *One of those who majors on minor "suggestions."*
> *Never anything big,*
> *Always telling you "a better way."*
> *"Now why don't you . . ."*
I guess it got to me;
> *I showed it.*
> *I shouldn't have.*

> Don't quarrel with anyone.
> Be at peace with everyone,
> just as much as possible
> (Rom. 12:18, TLB).

"You have the gift of getting along with people," one person says to another. "If I had that gift, there's nothing I couldn't do!"

Gift? Perhaps.

But in the majority of instances, it is not a gift, it is a purchase. The coin of exchange was time and effort. The basic materials bought might be recognition and responsibility.

The admonition to "Be at peace with everyone" slides easily off the tongue and slips into the sea of generalization. Perhaps it fits into the same category as "Have a nice day." Well meant, certainly, but involving no effort. Yet it is cut from different fabric. Being at peace with everyone does require effort on our part. Decidedly.

Notice again the last part of the verse, and the picture begins to emerge: ". . . just as much as possible." This tells me I have a personal involvement. I must bring "Be at peace" from the broad waters of generalization to the direct and directing river of personal responsibility.

As individuals, why do we react negatively at times when someone tells us what to do and how to do it? And what can we do about our reaction?

Perhaps the first thing is to step back emotionally. When I can get enough distance between the two of us, I see you as an individual . . . a person with your own ideas, even as I have mine. And then I need to remember what I have just said to myself: you are a person with ideas. Person. Ideas. These are separate. You and your ideas are not one and the same. I may react negatively to what you are saying without rejecting you as a person.

When we can internalize this concept that a person and his ideas are separate, our negative encounters are far less emotionally charged.

Jesus did this. Remember the rich young ruler? Seemingly, he could not do what Jesus asked, "Sell everything you have and give the money to the poor" (Matt. 19:21, TLB). He had a different idea, and he left. Jesus was saddened by his lack of understanding, but he loved him as a person.

A final step may be the most difficult of all. Is it possible that your idea is actually better than mine? It may be; it may not be. But I will not know until I separate myself from my feelings and weigh both ideas on the scale of objectivity. I do not need to be right to strengthen my personhood. I need to be open to have room to grow.

It does require effort. Getting along usually does.

10  Little Worries

Sometimes my days are darkened
By little worry clouds
> *Nagging at me,*
> *Hanging on.*
The big ones are different—
> *Thunder and lightning,*
> *Demanding attention.*
The little ones drift around
> *Almost silently,*
But they block the sunshine,
And the bright, the beautiful, becomes hazy.

> And now just as you trusted Christ to save you, trust him, too, for each day's problems; live in vital union with him (Col. 2:6, TLB).

A wealthy, middle-aged contractor, known to be a man of quick and decisive action, promptly went to the doctor in early January when a sudden and serious infection threatened his life. He was hospitalized and, upon returning home, faithfully followed the doctor's advice to ensure recovery.

A few months later, working on a personal project, he found a wooden splinter had broken off in the palm of his right hand. It was a small but irritating problem. The irritation dragged on while he and his wife vainly tried to remove the splinter.

"Why don't you go have the doctor get that thing out?" I asked, noticing how he favored his sore hand. "It may be just a splinter, but it looks like it's getting to be a problem."

He sighed, rubbing his hand. "It's a hassle all right. I just hate to bother a doctor with something as small as this."

Ultimately, he went to the doctor, and the problem was cleared up promptly.

Little worries . . . little?

The loving arm of the Lord is not limited to the eternal. It encircles our "every days" as well. If you can trust Christ with your eternal salvation, can't you trust him also to work out your everyday problems?

One might respond, "I never fully realized to what extent he is interested in everything about me, and that he really wants to lift the little worries off my shoulders and let me be free to live in the sunshine."

Another might say, "He's so big I think of him as involved in the eternal. I guess I forget that my todays are important to him, just like my eternity is."

A third might respond, "I know he can do it, but I just haven't stepped forward and taken him at his word. Maybe I'm too full of me, too self-sufficient. I think I can handle it, and I blow it."

Or a fourth, "I believe what the Bible says about taking all worries to the Lord, both the big ones and the little ones. What I need to do is do it! In other words, act upon it."

The contractor's hand could not function properly until the splinter was removed and the infection cleared up. We cannot function properly until the small worries that cloud our days are dissolved by God's omnipotent sunshine.

His promises are available not just by the asking, but by the taking. "Act upon it."

11  Impressing People

Something last week shook me up.
At a luncheon I sat next to a newcomer.
After a while I realized I was listening
To a litany of her accomplishments—
  All the things she had done,
  All the important people she knew.
The oldtimers fell silent.
  I felt sorry for the newcomer.
Then an uncomfortable thought began knocking
At the back door of my mind,
  "I wonder . . . Do I ever
  Subconsciously
  Try to impress people?
  Do I?"

Be of the same mind toward one another; do not be haughty in mind, but associate with the lowly. Do not be wise in your own estimation (Rom. 12:16, NASB).

My neighbor related this interesting experience.

"I was driving my new car, and I haven't used a stick shift in years. When I got ready to leave work, I thought I'd be going forward in first, but it turned out I went backward in reverse. Lucky for me, nothing was behind me!"

He was fortunate indeed. The problem surfaced immediately. Spiritually, it is sometimes more difficult to realize we are "in reverse." "Those who think themselves great shall be disappointed and humbled; and those who humble themselves shall be exalted" (Matt. 23:12, TLB).

Countless times the Bible warns us to beware of pride, one of those problems guaranteed to "throw us into reverse." We know this. Yet some of us have a pronounced tendency to make others aware of our friendships with important people and of our noteworthy accomplishments. The tendency is pronounced. Out loud, unfortunately. We may not do it in a direct manner, but we circle around the conversation until we see an opening, then with studied casualness we drop in a few well-chosen words.

There is a double irony here. The ones who are impressed are usually not the ones we are trying to cultivate; those who are not impressed sense what we are trying to do and react in reverse. The Bible is exactly right. Those who promote themselves will be humbled; those who humble themselves will be promoted.

Why can't we understand this? Usually we recognize that whatever talents we have come from the Lord, so that's not the problem. Perhaps we try to make ourselves look big because we feel small or inadequate. Consciously or subconsciously, we want to elevate ourselves by proving that we are worthwhile individuals. But personal adequacy is not evidenced by a recital of one's accomplishments or a listing of one's friends. It wells up from what a person is and bubbles to the outside. What you are results in what you accomplish and attracts those who become your friends. The world learns who we really are. It is shown, not told.

There are times when words flail the air and go nowhere. Or worse, sometimes they hit the wrong target. They throw a relationship into reverse. There are also times when a nonverbal communication shouts the truth. Loudly. Ultimately, the world listens. Assuming, of course, there is something to be heard. Maybe this should be our first concern.

12  Burnout

I don't know when I've felt so tired,
    Drugged with fatigue.
But somewhere through the fog, a wisp of a
thought nags at my consciousness.
    Am I really this tired
    Or is it part discouragement?
    Plain vanilla blues?
Maybe I'm "tired of" more than "tired"—
Tired of carrying the ball,
    Keeping on keeping on,
    When others don't seem to care.
Is that it?

> Being confident of this very thing, that he which hath begun a good work in you will perform it until the day of Jesus Christ (Phil. 1:6).

Striking out is not confined to the baseball diamond. And burnout is becoming increasingly common in today's fast-paced society. From the corporation executive to the volunteer church worker, no area can claim immunity. In talking with some who have had this problem, we find several responses.

"I just got tired of the rat race. I can't see that I'm accomplishing anything."

"It got to be a twenty-four-hour-a-day job. It's just not worth it. Life is more than that or should be."

"I don't know why I should keep on knocking myself out when no one else seems to care."

These comments point up what seem to be two basic factors in burnout. We are tempted to give up when we carry too much for too long without visible results; the desire to give up is stronger when we feel we are fighting the battle alone. Sometimes these factors stack up. And the stack is too high to hurdle. It need not be so.

Most of us would say that to work long and hard is not a problem if we feel our labor is worthwhile and if we can see affirming results. Herein lies one of the problems. We are visually oriented. To see positive results is pleasant, even helpful, but is it essential? Cannot we trust God with the outcome?

In the second area, "feeling alone in the north forty," we may have a similar problem. A job is easier if we are involved in a team effort. Sports history sparkles with stories of teams whose togetherness made the difference. But aloneness is something else. Could it be that we are reverting back to our visually oriented patterns again and seeking visible support? Although we may not have physical co-workers, we have something far better. We have Someone far better.

God, who began the work, will keep right on working in you, through you, all the way to victory.

You don't have to see results.

You don't have to struggle alone.

Not now. Not ever.

 Overcoming

13   Go for It!

I read about Catherine Marshall
    Or Margaret Thatcher
    Or Beverly Sills
And I think "Wow!
    She's way up there."
Then someone in my town wins a short story contest,
    And my neighbor down the street paints a landscape,
And I am impressed,
    Even awed.
She's another one with talent and ability.
    I'm just me
    Down here.

As God's messenger I give each of you God's warning: Be honest in your estimate of yourselves, measuring your value by how much faith God has given you. . . . God has given each of us the ability to do certain things well (Rom. 12:3,6a, TLB).

Laura worked as a reporter for a daily paper in California during the days when the Hollywood Canteen, a USO for servicemen, was opened. Visiting in the area on opening night, she saw the evening sky split with yellow shafts of light and hundreds of excited fans milling around the canteen entrance to catch a glimpse of the stars.

My friend, new to her job and new to California as well, joined the masses. Being a novice in the popular pastime of star gazing, she found herself pushed back farther and farther from the gates.

Suddenly she thought, *What am I doing back here? I have a press pass. No one else from my paper is here, and I could be covering this!* She dug into her purse for her credentials and elbowed through the crowd. The policeman at the gate glanced at her press pass and waved her through.

It all happened so suddenly she couldn't quite believe it. "Why did I waste time struggling outside when I could have been inside with the rest of the reporters?"

Why indeed?

Each of us has abilities; each needs to be honest in examining and evaluating that which we have. God's children are all made from the same material. Those who impress us the most are still simply people.

The difference between those who have reached the top and others may be twofold; they have used the capabilities God gave them and have done so persistently. Perhaps we have not, as yet. We owe achievers our respect; we do not owe them adulation.

Sometimes we admire others so much that we make ourselves small by comparison. That's unhealthy for them and belittling for us. They become more than life-size; we become pygmies.

Certainly we cannot say that with persistence we could have become a Chris Evert Lloyd or a Katharine Hepburn. Talents are obviously different. But is it not true that we could find as much satisfaction in using our capabilities as they do in theirs? Is not true fulfillment found in the maximum use of God-given abilities, whatever they be?

I have a spiritual press pass. So do you.

14  Crossroads

The day brims with excitement,
A new opportunity.
>   *Hey, this is great, let's get started.*
>   *We can do this . . . and this . . . and . . .*
Then something deep within me begins to gnaw,
>   *How do I know it will work?*
>   *Maybe I'll get slapped down again.*
>   *Who do I think I am?*
And my enthusiasm dribbles away.
I am perplexed, confused,
>   *Wanting to surge forward, yet held back*
>   *By the soft, strong cords of yesterday.*

> "But this one thing I do, forgetting those things which are behind, and reaching forth unto those which are before, I press toward the mark for the prize of the high calling of God in Christ Jesus" (Phil. 3:13-14).

The frisky brown dog, leashed to the tree, discovered the old shoe and pounced on it. First, he stretched out on the ground with the bedraggled loafer between his paws and gnawed at it. Then he jumped up and, with a toss of his head, flung the shoe several feet away. He eyed it, then scampered after it.

But he forgot his leash. Suddenly, at full speed, he was jerked off his feet as the leash pulled taut. Startled rather than hurt, he rolled over and looked around in confusion. Earlier, he had been leashed because of the city ordinance. He was still tied.

And so it is with us, at times. We forget that the leash, fastened at some previous point, may still be tied. If it inhibits our forward progress, it needs to be loosened or loosed.

In yesterday's world, the experiences and relationships that touched us also molded us and, in that molding, left a part of themselves. Most of the time, we have moved on, knowing ourselves to be a part of all that we have met, yet trailing no constricting ties that bind us and pull us backwards.

It is not that we are ungrateful. There is appreciation for lessons learned in the universal school of experience and gratitude for those who invested their yesterdays for our todays. We owe much, but we do not pay our debt by recurring reflection. We must live out our gratitude.

Unfortunately, in some instances, we cling to the past or permit it to cling to us. We remember our mistakes, our disappointments, our limited abilities needlessly. We hold fast to relationships when only a shell remains, or lean on past honors chronicled only in fading plaques.

If we will pull our lingering glance from the past and deliberately look around us, we will see that today's machines cannot be made from yesterday's blueprints. Modern equipment may have evolved from earlier models, but each one has been adjusted in line with today's demands and tomorrow's needs. The world moves forward.

On a personal level, we cannot move forward while looking backward. "Forgetting those things which are behind . . . I press [forward]."

Remembering . . .

"This is the day the Lord hath made."

15  Bitterness

She came to me, crestfallen,
*   Her eyes dark with pain,*
And flopped into my kitchen chair.
"I can't believe I did that . . ."
*   She paused, then went on,*
"We were having a committee meeting
*   And Clara was there.*
*   You remember Clara?*
*   We had a bad run-in year before last.*
Something she said today hit me wrong,
*   Went all over me.*
Before I knew it, I lashed out,
*   Told her off from A to Z*
*   Just like a dam broke.*
I can't believe I did that . . ."

See to it that no one comes short of the grace of God; that no root of bitterness springing up causes trouble, and by it many be defiled (Heb. 12:15, NASB).

"Did you get all the roots out?" A friend curiously surveyed the area his next-door neighbor had cleared to build a patio.

"Most of them," came the reply. "The big ones, anyway. What's left is so small it won't make any difference." But it did.

Months later, the concrete poured for the patio began to crack and break, jutting up in jagged pieces. The small roots that wouldn't make any difference had become sturdy and powerful. Bit by bit, they exerted increasing pressure until even the hardened concrete had broken.

Ruptured relationships seldom jut into our lives full grown. But rather the seed was planted, and the roots came into being some remembered yesterday. That was the problem. Yesterday, remembered. We nourished the bitter root by giving it memory time. We kept it alive and growing until finally one day it broke the concrete of our composure and we were stunned.

"I can't believe I said that (or did that)!" We are aghast. We need not be. Remembering can work for us or against us. That which we ponder will grow. The captive thought we refuse to relinquish may ultimately become captor.

Roots, unfortunately, have no ethics. The bad ones grow right along with the good ones. We have both in our minds. The ones that grow are the ones we nourish by deliberation. When we follow the admonition to let love, joy, peace, dwell within, these will be the ones to root and grow.

A bitter pill may be ours to swallow, but it need not become rooted. We have the choice, but the action to remove it must be deliberate.

God can and will take the bitterness away. It is easier to do before it becomes rooted, but it can be done any step along the way. The plan seems so simple that, like Naaman of old when told to wash in the Jordan seven times, we disbelieve. Involved in the process are asking God to remove the bitterness, believing he can do it, and replacing the bitter thoughts with loving ones.

Remember, loving thoughts can take root also. And the captive again becomes the captor. Praise the Lord.

16  The Other Cheek

First I was incredulous, stunned.
  I don't think it happened.
Then I was hurt.
  How could she think that?
  Let alone say it!
  I thought we were friends.
  I guess I was wrong.
Now anger churns my insides,
  Red flames whipping up.
Now I want to confront her,
  Tell her she's wrong,
  Whittle her down.
  Now. Right now.

> Do not let evil defeat you;
> instead, conquer evil with
> good (Rom. 12:21, GNB).

The look of pain in her eyes surprised me, perhaps because I so seldom saw it there. She was usually a cheerful, happy person, the kind who is well able to "take the lemons that life brings and make lemonade."

"Do you want to tell me about it?" I asked casually, hoping to give her the opportunity to share her problem.

She sat quietly for a moment, folding and unfolding a paper napkin with long, slender fingers. "Mostly, I'm thinking about how the good and the bad sometimes go together," she said. "You know, like they're a part of the same package. Maybe there are times you can't have one without the other."

I waited a moment, then she continued.

"I enjoy teaching, and I especially enjoy trying to help students with special problems. And I have one boy like that right now. He's been in the hospital so much of his young life that he has a problem keeping up, and I don't think it's going to get any better soon. At any rate, he's a joy to work with this semester. On the other side of the picture, I've finished my master's degree in administration, and I'm up for the principal's job in the new elementary school next fall."

Again, silence.

"And that's a problem?" I asked after a bit.

She shook her head. "That's just the prologue. Here's what's happening. The boy I'm helping is the son of the school board president. One of my co-workers has also applied for the new job, and she's saying that I only work with the boy because I'm trying to butter up his father and that I'll probably help even more as the spring goes on."

"And will you?"

She smiled wryly. "Yes, I will. That's where the good and the bad both come in. The woman, who was my friend, will go right on talking about me, and that's bad. And I'll go right on helping the boy because he needs it and because I enjoy it. And that's good."

"I admire you."

"Don't." She shook her head firmly. "I'm just an implementer. I truly believe that God's good . . . ministry . . . conquers evil."

An implementer. It's also called life-style Christianity.

 Consistency

17  Handling Disappointments

Today my problems came in duplicates,
  And I wasn't prepared.
First, my cochairman didn't show up to work,
  And I was surprised.
  I was hurt.
  I was left holding the bag.
Later in the day, the phone rang—
A second disappointment,
  "Did you know that . . .?"
  No, I didn't,
  More pieces to pick up.
Really now,
Whatever happened to responsibility?
What kind of Christianity is this?

> They are God's servants, not yours. They are responsible to him, not to you (Rom. 14:4, TLB).

Do one and one still add up to two? Maybe. It depends on the person doing the adding.

Certainly the human equation defies consistency. What seems like simple addition or elementary logic to one person does not to another. Identical input does not yield identical results in the human arena. We are not machines; we are people. And the processing is different.

"Of course, I know you don't think as I do," my friend said in jest. "And certainly you have a right to your own ridiculous opinion!"

We smile; but deep down inside, how do we feel about it? While we may not go so far as to label another's ideas as "ridiculous," we sometimes find ourselves surprised, even hurt, when another person does not think or perform as we would in the same circumstances. In fact, at times we are devastated.

What is our problem? Perhaps we are bounded and hounded on all sides by our own opinions and concepts. The idea of walking in someone else's moccasins before we form opinions about his conduct is both widely known and widely disregarded. To step into another's shoes is only partially possible; it may happen if both come from similar backgrounds and have had similar experiences. Otherwise it is difficult, indeed.

But there are some avenues not only open to us but also recommended. We can begin by accepting the fact that the person who has "defaulted" is coming from a different place: she is influenced by the sum total of her own experiences, even as we are by ours. Next, we can recognize that the area involved may be a problem area for her: she may be unable to accept responsibility or to follow through. We have weaknesses in other areas. She may be working on her problem and, therefore, needing our support rather than our criticism, spoken or unspoken.

Underlying and overlaying the entire situation may be the most important fact of all, and one that too often eludes us. Part of the problem may be within us. I need to remember that I am responsible only for my own performance, not that of someone else.

I am not the general chairman of the world.

God is.

18  Second Wind

Another day. Same song, third verse,
  Except the date is different.
Sometimes I feel like a robot—
Just doing what needs to be done—
  Push a button and I'll go into my routine.
  But sometimes it's hard to find the button.
  "Button, button, who's got the button?"
  I don't.
There's just so much of it.
But it's all cut from the same cloth.
  Or maybe it's all layered over with sameness,
  Sameness . . . Sameness.

> Never be lazy in your work but serve the Lord enthusiastically (Rom. 12:11, TLB).

Enthusiasm is like the morning sun peeking over the mountaintop. First you see it, then you begin to feel it, and soon you're radiating its warmth.

Each of us can recall instances when someone walked in the room and sunshine came in with her. She glowed; she was a magnet. And before we ever knew her or the cause she espoused, we were pulled halfway through the gate by the sheer force of another's enthusiasm.

Often this is our experience when we begin a new job, assume a new task, or enter a new relationship. We believe in what we are doing; it shows. But after a while the glow fades, and we find ourselves plodding along instead of perking. We are lulled into monotony by the overlapping sameness of our days.

What has happened? We had felt called to a particular type of service, but we're not happy. What's wrong?

It may be decision time. God may be calling us elsewhere. Or it may be something else: we may be looking at the immediate routine and not the ultimate result, insofar as God has shown it to us.

In the beginning, we saw our assignment as helping, as contributing, or we would not have begun it. We approached it with zest because of what it could do. We kept our eyes on what we were attempting to accomplish. The process was secondary, a means to an end.

And now? Perhaps we have become enmeshed in the everydayness that is a part of every worthwhile task or relationship. The mundane routines have loomed larger and larger by the sheer weight of hours given to them. We're out of balance.

We need to view or visualize the end result along with the routines of the day. The painter must be involved in detail, but he must also step back to view the total canvas or lose his perspective. So must we.

Let's look again. The task is there. Observe the opportunities it gives us for reaching out and touching, for building and helping to build, for giving someone an extra boost so that he may see a new horizon. And remember, you're the one whom God is working through to accomplish it. That's exciting. Let your excitement show. It's contagious.

19 The Time Factor

Today's schedule staggers me,
And I haven't even started.
It's not just crammed full,
It's running over.
Running.
That list is not running,
I am.
How did I ever get in this shape?
Too much to do,
And what do I leave off?
I can't keep running without refueling
And there's no time,
No time . . . no time.

Then Jesus suggested, 'Let's get away from the crowds for a while and rest.' For so many people were coming and going that they scarcely had time to eat. So they left by boat for a quieter spot (Mark 6:31-32, TLB).

Sometimes our days become so clogged with activity that there is no breathing room or "being" room. Without the fresh air of uncluttered time, a few islands for refueling, we become race cars rather than persons, ricocheting around the oval of one day and plunging into another. "The tyranny of the urgent" gobbles up our days. But is it all urgent? By whose standards?

Certainly to the friend who asked you to head up the subscription drive, the matter is urgent. And to the one who enlisted you to help with the arts and crafts show, the matter is vital. These are good projects. But before you accept, have you blocked out the time on your calendar?

Perhaps the matter turns on the key word *acceptance*. We can do little to lighten today's schedule, but we can take action now to structure tomorrow's differently. The seed we plant today, the responsibilities we accept, will most certainly sprout tomorrow. Another factor is that plants have a way of growing to a prescribed size; responsibilities have a way of mushrooming.

"I'll accept any engagement if you ask me a year in advance," an area speaker said in jest. But the truth of the statement is abundantly clear as we look at our calendars today. Emergencies do arise; but for the most part, we are put on the fast track by promissory notes made yesterday. Today they have come due.

The Bible tells us that Jesus took time apart. If the One who was and is the Master of all circumstances blocked out personal time, if he deemed it needful, how can we possibly function at our best without it?

Two suggestions may be helpful. First, block out "personal time" the same way you block out engagements or responsibilities, and hold these as inviolate as the commitments made to others. Second, to determine what to accept and what to decline, make your priorities a matter of prayer, and write the list down. Include your personal time, along with family, church, and professional responsibilities, depending on your life structure. Now add those extras you feel led to accept, but avoid scheduling "back to back." Most responsibilities take more time to fulfill than we anticipate.

Neither the "tyranny of the urgent" nor the nibbles of everydayness should devour our days. Time is for living.

20 Stability

For a moment it seemed almost unreal:
The fairgrounds in slow motion,
> *Thinning crowds,*
> *Daylight darkening into rosy dusk.*
Lights came on,
> *Splashing color across the midway.*
Then I saw the roller coaster in the distance
Its train of tiny cars inching upward,
> *Cresting at the top,*
> *Hurdling down*
> *Up again, down again—*
And the sense of unreality left me.
> *This is the real world.*
I have a friend with that problem—
> *Up, down.*
She absorbs whatever is tossed at her;
> *So she's up, then down.*

> God has made us what we
> are, and in our union with
> Christ Jesus he has created
> us for a life of good deeds
> (Eph. 2:10, GNB).

When I saw her at noon she was bright and cheerful, her blue eyes sparkling as she told me about her upcoming activities. Later that afternoon, our paths accidentally crossed again. But she was quiet and subdued and had an aura of sadness about her.

"What happened?" I knew her well enough to ask. "You were bubbling over at noontime. Did your plans fall apart?"

She shook her head. "No, not really. In fact, it has nothing to do with the things we talked about. I've been in another meeting this afternoon, and one of the women in that group always criticizes. It's subtle, but it's there. I just can't do anything right. It gets me down."

That is sad and needless. Obviously neither a clutter of compliments nor a diet of darts is healthy, although a selection of each may be offered on our daily menu. We hear, but we do not need to absorb. There's a big difference.

Comments made to you or about you may be justified. They may not. You'll have to decide. But if the statement is untrue, remember that the verbalizing of it does not cause it to become truth. Dismiss it. Nothing is changed. On any given Monday, you may call it Tuesday all day long, but that will not make it Tuesday. By the same token, when verbal bickerings or brick-bats come your way, nothing need be changed, unless you permit it.

Words are to be filtered, not swallowed. If the filtration process shows them to be true, ingest them. If not, let them flow by. The stream of conversation seldom lacks for adequate springs. Words are in abundance. Comments coming your way will go around you unless you choose to catch them.

Essentially, you are you—a child of God, made in his image and given special capabilities. You are to interact with others, to minister. But you cannot do it on a roller coaster, up one minute and down the next, your stability dependent upon whatever words may be swirling in the atmosphere about you.

You are you. God made you, strengthens you, stabilizes you. Rejoice.

God's Presence

21  Worship

He's up there preaching, a guest in my church.
  He looks right, he sounds right.
Everyone seems to be listening,
  Except me
  And a small boy in the second row.
I'm having trouble—
There's a curtain between the preacher and me
  Woven from remembered incidents.
What he says and what he does are not consistent,
  And it bothers me.
Yet I need to worship, I need to,
  I truly need to.

"But Lord," exclaimed Ananias, "I have heard about the terrible things this man has done to the believers in Jerusalem." . . . But the Lord said, "Go and do what I say. For Paul is my chosen instrument" (Acts 9:13,15, TLB).

"What exactly do we mean when we say *worship*?"

This question, posed to a roomful of young adults, brought forth a variety of responses.

"It means to put everything else out of your mind and think about God."

"It means waiting in awe before God and thanking him for

all he has done. It is communication."

One response was a two-word definition: "Worship is *soul food.*"

Each of us would answer the question a little differently, but each would agree on one thing: the need for worship experiences on a regular basis, soul food.

Maybe too many of us are on self-imposed diets. Perhaps the diet craze that floods our consciousness from newpapers, magazines, and TV alike has seeped under the door of our worship room. We are imposing limits on our spiritual intake by diluting or filtering the menu. The time frame is the same, but the fare is far less nourishing because we are seeing the messengers as individuals.

"The door to my worship room has three steps," said an older woman. "I must go up them one at a time, no skipping. And if I do, I can count on a worship experience."

For her the steps were to put everything else out of her mind and to open herself to God's message in the Scripture, the music, and the sermon. She concentrates on seeing the persons involved as instruments, not individuals. "If you see them as people," she explained, "you may be bothered by an off-key note or two, a mispronounced word, or a sermon that doesn't ring true all the way. That will dilute your worship time. You need it full strength."

Then, with a clear and concentrating mind, she listens. "To listen is to be actively open to what's going on and let it speak to you. It's different from just hearing. Somewhere in the service you'll find a message designed especially for you, although all of it might not parallel your own thinking."

Her third step is to use the invitation as a personal response time. "I pray for those in the service and I pray for myself, that I might act upon what God has brought to my consciousness. And I leave the church refreshed in spirit." That is worship.

22 "Go with Me, God"

I remember reading a funny story—
   A man jumped on his horse
   And "rode madly off in all directions."
Well, I've done him one better—
   I'm going madly off in all directions
   Without a horse.
But it's not the "all directions" that bothers me.
   Needs are needs,
   Regardless of geography.
It's just that I can't nail anything down,
   Finish it, cross it off my list.
Things keep coming loose, coming undone,
   Or maybe it's me
   Coming undone.
I need to go out and come in again.

> I love them that love me; and those that seek me early shall find me (Prov. 8:17).

The small family, involved in many phases of the church program, was frequently the last to leave the church on Sunday morning. As they made their way toward the exit, the custodian followed and carefully locked the massive front doors behind them.

The little boy, reaching up for his mother's hand, called out cheerfully, "Good-bye, God, I'll see you next week!"

Is worship, the practice of the presence of God, a part of our daily lives or apart from our lives? Do we come away from the place of prayer feeling like, *Well, that's done. Now I can get on with living,* or do we recognize the need for carrying God into that living on an hourly basis?

"After my prayer time, it's time to move forward into my day," the career woman said. "I remind myself that God goes before me, with me, and that he's there after I have moved down the road. He doesn't need me to make the path. I need him to find it.

"I've made myself develop the habit of remembering his presence. I'm a working woman; I believe my vocation is of the Lord. Since I know he has called me to this area of work, I must get out of my prayer closet and move along, but I must bring him with me. Maybe I ought to phrase that another way. I don't need to bring him anywhere. He's already there. What I need to do is affirm his presence in such a way that my thoughts, my behavior, reflect the fact that he is there. It makes a world of difference in me and my day. Worship, you know, is not confined to the church on Sunday mornings."

Affirming God's presence does not mean the doors will swing open automatically all day long. They may; they may not. It does not mean you will never be frustrated, angry, hurt, or disappointed. You will. But the fabric of your day will be different because you have shifted the weaving to Someone else. Someone greater than you is present, the Master Weaver. It is not "Good-bye, God, I'll see you next week." But rather it is "Good morning, God. I'm grateful we have another day to travel together."

Being in God's presence makes for a totally different journey.

23  Comes the Harvest

I peer into the scalloped flower beds
    Edging the front of the house
    Shaded by sturdy oak trees.
Eagerly my eyes scan the soil
    Moist with remembered rain,
    Rich brown earth
    Still unbroken by the timid thrustings of new life.
Where are the tiny blades that should be peeking out
    To stretch upward,
    To bloom in colorful profusion?
I know I prepared the earth, planted, watered.
    Where are the flowers?

> Let us not be weary in well doing: for in due season we shall reap, if we faint not (Gal. 6:9).

"You're the answer to my prayers," the front of the friendship card said. Then the inside had a slightly different message: "Well, you're not exactly what I prayed for, but apparently you're the answer!"

When harvest time comes, the reaping of that which we have sowed, it may loom on the horizon in recognizable form; it may not. Yet God's word is true. The harvest does come.

"There are times when I get so discouraged," a good friend said. "I feel like I'm doing all I possibly can at home, at church, and in our town. But I can't see that I'm getting anywhere. Does there ever come a time when you see results?"

Yes, but sometimes results are slow in appearing. It takes patience embedded in faith to await the sprouting of the seed sowed on fertile soil. And sometimes when the harvest comes, we are not aware of it. At other times, it is beautifully and blessedly apparent.

A widow of less than average means struggled to provide her daughter with not only the basic material needs but also a strong personal faith and moral convictions. She even found a way to send the young woman to college, although it meant additional personal sacrifice.

After the daughter left, weeks went by with short letters giving news of academics and activities. But, as the mother related it, nothing was said about "how things were going on the inside."

Then one day late in autumn, a special letter came. "I'm sitting here alone tonight in my room," the daughter wrote. "I have some thoughts I want to share with you."

The letter recalled some incidents of early childhood and then continued: "Because of you, I came to know Jesus at an early age and to let him be Lord of my life. Because of you, I had everything I really needed materially, although I know it wasn't easy. And you always found time to spend with me and to instill in me those standards you live by.

"Since I have been here, I've really found out that many people don't hold those standards. But I know what I believe and why I believe it. At times it's tough, but I have my head on straight.

"I get all teary when I try to write about it, but they are tears of gratitude. I just want to say . . . 'Thanks, Mom.'"

The harvest comes.

24 The Giver

The package sparkles under the Christmas tree;
    Glittering,
    Star-spangled,
    Picking up the lights dancing above.
I pick it up curiously, carefully,
    And turn it over in my hands;
    Slowly, gently,
    Afraid to shake it
I don't know what the gift is,
    But I really don't need to.
    It could be any number of things.
I do know it will be just right,
Because I know the giver.

> For God so loved . . . that he gave (John 3:16a).

"Look, Daddy, I made you a gift! And I worked on it all day long!"

It was Christmastime, and the little girl's eyes sparkled as she handed the childishly wrapped package to her father. "Open it now," she pleaded, almost jumping up and down in her excitement. "I know it's not Christmas yet, but I want you to open it right now!"

The father reached for the child before he opened the gift. "Whatever it is, if you made it, Honey, I know I'll like it." He hugged her and then began to unfasten the bulky string that held the flat package.

Inside was a rectangular white placard, the edges painted

green, and a mixture of unreadable red letters in the center.

"You can read it, can't you?" the child asked anxiously. "It says 'I love you.' I made it without anybody helping me!"

The father, his eyes misting, looked down at the scrambled letters. "Of course, I can read it," he responded. "Love is a language everybody can understand. We call it 'universal.'"

Indeed, love could be no other than a universal language since it is both epitomized and spoken by the One who made the universe.

Love is more than a feeling; it is a force. It moves from formlessness to form. It forces its way through the shapeless mists of feeling into visible and viable forms called action.

God who loves also gives. He is the perfect Giver. His gifts come shaped to fit the specific individual and the existing circumstances. Additionally, each gift arrives at the exact point in time when it is needed in accordance with omniscient wisdom.

Sometimes when the gift arrives we can read it perfectly. On other occasions, like the earthly father, we must know that the gift says "I love you" although we can neither read it nor understand it.

Today's vision may be blurred.

Tomorrow's will be clearer when time and spiritual stature give us taller perspective.

God is the perfect Giver.

Always.